OUR CLOTHES

LEATHER SHOES

Wayne Jackman

Reading Consultant:
Diana Bentley
University of Reading

Commissioned photographs:
Chris Fairclough

07539

Wayland

Our clothes

Denim Jeans
Leather Shoes
Nylon Tracksuit
Plastic Raincoat
Woolly Hat

Editor: Janet De Saulles

First published in 1990 by
Wayland (Publishers) Ltd
61 Western Road, Hove
East Sussex, BN3 1JD, England

© Copyright 1990 Wayland (Publishers) Ltd

British Library Cataloguing in Publication Data
Jackman, Wayne
  Leather shoes
  1. Leather clothing. Making
  I. Title II. Fairclough, Chris. III. Series
  646.4

  ISBN 1–85210–855–X

Phototypeset by Rachel Gibbs, Wayland
Printed and bound by Casterman S.A., Belgium

Contents

All the words that appear in **bold** are explained in the glossary on page 22.

Above *These children are all wearing shoes made from leather.*

Leather is best

Are you wearing any shoes at the moment? Millions of pairs of shoes are made in factories every year! Most of these are made from leather. Leather is very strong. It protects our feet and it can also bend easily without breaking. It lets the air get to our feet, keeping our skin healthy. Even with our modern inventions we have not found anything better to make our shoes with.

Right *There are many different styles of shoe. Some shoes are done up with a buckle and some with laces.*

Have you ever wondered where leather comes from? It comes from the skins of animals, such as buffalos and cows, or sheep or pigs.

Above *We get leather from animals such as these cows from Kenya.*

Cleaning and tanning the skins

After the skins have been removed from the dead animals they are put in salty water. This helps the hairs on the surface of the skins to fall away. The skins, or **hides**, are then thoroughly washed to remove all the dirt.

To stop the skins from drying out they are **tanned**. A person called a **tanner** puts the skins into large drums. These have a special liquid in them called **tannin**. The tannin soaks into the skins to **preserve** them. Soap and oil can later be rubbed on to keep the skins bendy and supple. The skins then look like the leather we know.

A close-up view

Each piece of leather has two layers. These are separated before being used. The outer layer is called full grain leather. The inner layer is called suede leather. Both can be used to make shoes but the full grain leather is more popular because it is **waterproof**.

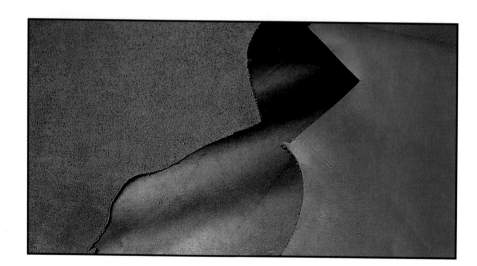

Right Can you see the difference between the red suede leather and the blue and black full grain leather?

Left *These French shoes have been dyed lovely bright colours.*

Below *These drums are full of dye.*

Before being made into shoes the leather is often **dyed**. The leather is dipped in big drums full of dye. It is important that the dyeing is done well, otherwise the colour will rub off on to our socks.

Designing the shoes

Shoe factories have **designers** who decide what the shoes should look like. They often use computers to help them design the shape of the shoe and any patterns that will go on the new shoe.

Above *This shoe designer must decide what style, shape and colour the new shoes will be.*

Right *The shoes here are being designed on a computer.*

10

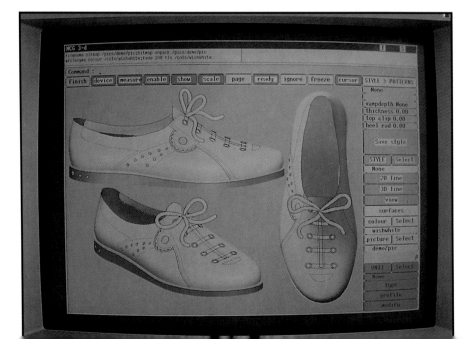

Look at the picture showing the parts of a shoe. All these have to be designed, cut out and put together before a shoe is ready to wear. There can be as many as thirty parts to a shoe.

Below This picture shows the different parts that are needed to make a shoe.

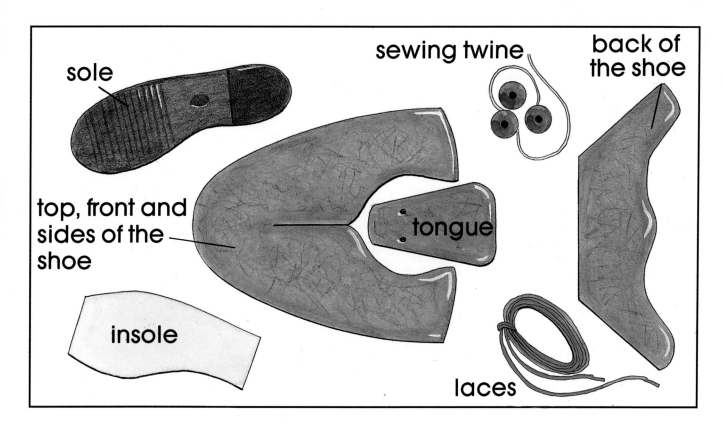

sole

sewing twine

back of the shoe

top, front and sides of the shoe

tongue

insole

laces

Cutting the leather

Above *Many shoes, especially training shoes, have soles which are made of plastic.*

Opposite page *The leather is cut very carefully so that hardly any is wasted.*

At last the leather arrives at the factory. It is first inspected for good quality. Then it is sent to the **cutting room**. A cutter or **clicker** lays out each leather skin. The clicker uses a machine called a **press** to cut out the different parts of the shoe. The clicker is very good at this and wastes hardly any leather.

The soles of the shoes usually are made from a variety of plastics. This is because they have a better grip than leather. Melted plastic is poured into a **mould** and allowed to set hard. Each different style or shoe size needs its own mould.

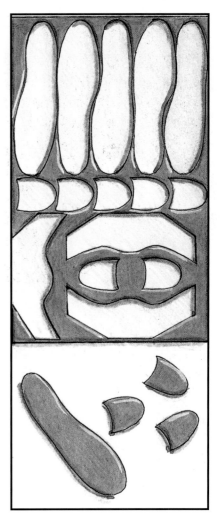

Above *Some of the different shapes the leather is cut into.*

13

Making the upper part of the shoe

The clicker sends the cut out pieces of leather to the **closing room**. Here the upper part of the shoe is stitched together. Fast electric sewing machines are used for this job.

A piece of metal shaped like a person's foot is then put into the leather upper part of the shoe. This piece of metal is called a last. The whole thing is heated so that the leather is moulded to the shape of the last. Finally an **insole** is stuck to the bottom of the upper with a strong glue. The shoe is now taking shape.

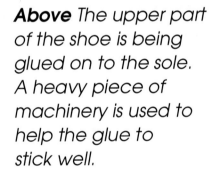 # Finishing off the shoes

The shoe making process is now finished off. The soles and the uppers are stuck together with more strong glue. Sometimes they are also stitched for added strength.

Above *The upper part of the shoe is being glued on to the sole. A heavy piece of machinery is used to help the glue to stick well.*

Finally, the last is taken out. The shoes are now matched up in pairs and go to the shoe room. Here, the shoes are given the final touches. Eyelets and laces are added, the shoes are polished and an insock is added. Then the shoes are packed into boxes ready to be sent to the shops and be sold to the customers.

Left *While one shoe is being pressed, the next shoe is taken and a sole glued to it.*

Below *Once the shoes are finished they are packed into boxes.*

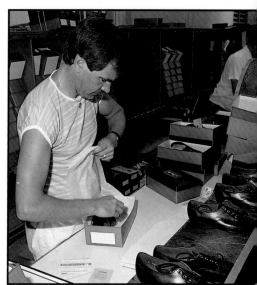

17

These pictures show how leather is made into shoes.

The shoes reach the shops

All sorts of shops sell shoes. Perhaps you have bought some in a specialized shoe shop or maybe a department store. Have you ever had your feet measured to see what size they are? This is important to help your feet grow healthily.

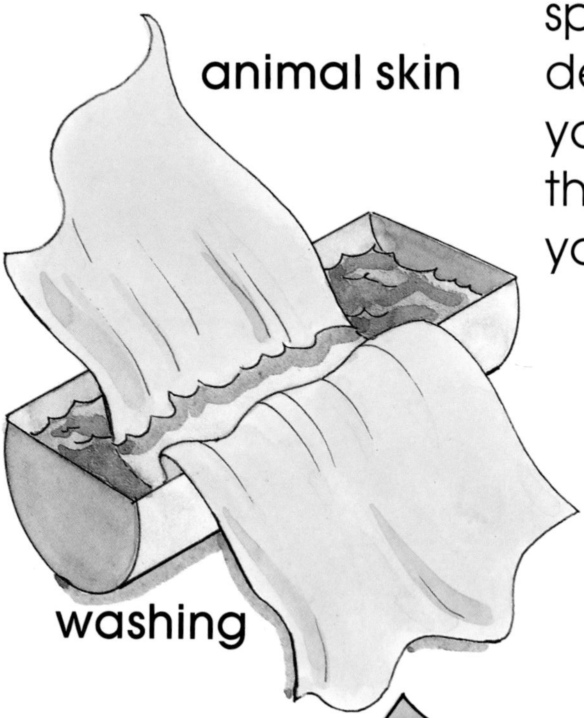

animal skin

washing

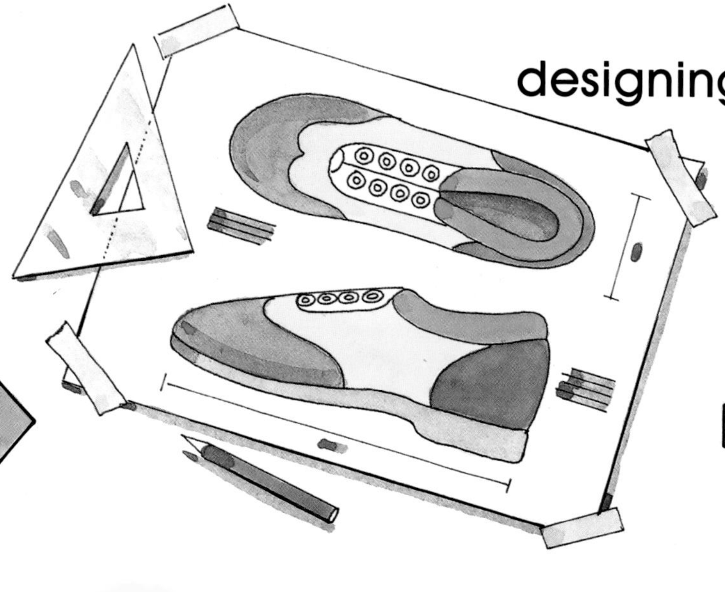

designing

Some countries have a long **tradition** of hand-making leather shoes. In Morocco, Spain and Greece you might see a market stall selling this type of shoe.

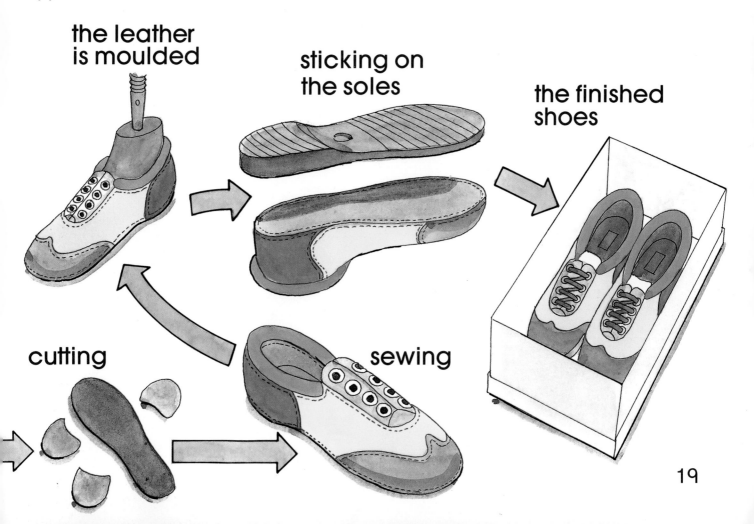

the leather is moulded

sticking on the soles

the finished shoes

cutting

sewing

19

Your own shoes

Look at your own shoes carefully. Are they made of leather? Perhaps they are made of canvas or plastic. You can usually tell leather by the way it looks or feels. Try examining the pattern on the outside of the shoes.

Below Next time you put on your shoes, see if you can tell what they are made from.

Left *One way of testing leather is by smelling it. Nothing else smells quite like leather.*

Below *How much shine can you get on your shoes?*

If your shoes get wet it is best to stuff them with newspaper and let them dry naturally. It is also a good idea to polish your leather shoes. This will keep them supple and smart. It will help them to last longer too!

Glossary

Clicker   Nickname for the person who cuts out the leather shapes.

Closing room   This is the place where the upper part of the shoe is stitched together.

Cutting Room   Where the leather is cut into shapes for the parts of the shoe.

Designers   People whose job it is to invent and draw out new styles of shoes.

Dyed   When something is given a new colour.

Hides   The skins of large animals such as buffalos or cows.

Insole   The part of the shoe sandwiched between the sole and the upper.

Mould   Molten plastic is poured into a mould. When the plastic has become hard, it has the same shape as the mould.

Preserve   To keep something fresh and new looking.

Press   A machine which presses a shape cutter into the leather to cut out shapes.

Tanned   When the animals' skins have been soaked to make them bendy and long-lasting.

Tanner   The person who carries out the tanning.

Tannin   A substance found in plants which changes new hides or skins into leather.

Tradition   Something that has been done for many years.

Waterproof   Keeps out water.

Books to read

How Clothes are Made by Sue Crawford (Wayland, 1987)

How it's Made: Clothing and Footwear by Donald Clarke (Marshall Cavendish, 1978)

Making Shoes by Ruth Thomson (Franklin Watts, 1986)

The Wonderful Story of Leather by K J Beeby (The Leather Institute)

Index

Acknowledgements

The author and Publisher would like to thank C and J Clark for their kind permission in allowing the commissioned photographs to be taken at their Somerset shoe factory.

They would also like to thank the following for allowing illustrations to be reproduced in this book: Connolly Leather 6, 9 (right); Trevor Hill 20; Kickers 9 (left); Paul Seheult 21; Wayland Picture Library 5, 7; 12. The illustrations on pages 11, 13, 18 and 19 are by Stephen Wheele.